P9-BYW-685

PALATINE P...

8026

Nov 2015

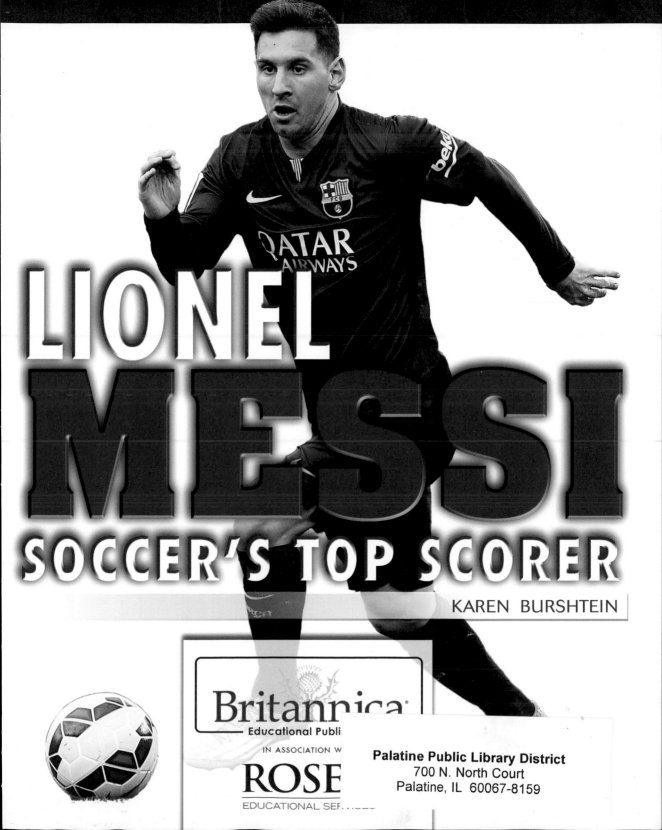

LIONEL MESSI
SOCCER'S TOP SCORER

KAREN BURSHTEIN

Britannica
Educational Publi

IN ASSOCIATION W

ROSE
EDUCATIONAL SER

Palatine Public Library District
700 N. North Court
Palatine, IL 60067-8159

To Caitie Burshtein and Charlotte and Sarah Kowall

Published in 2016 by Britannica Educational Publishing (a trademark of Encyclopædia Britannica, Inc.) in association with The Rosen Publishing Group, Inc.
29 East 21st Street, New York, NY 10010

Copyright © 2016 The Rosen Publishing Group, Inc., and Encyclopædia Britannica, Inc. Encyclopædia Britannica, Britannica, and the Thistle logo are registered trademarks of Encyclopædia Britannica, Inc. All rights reserved.

Distributed exclusively by Rosen Publishing.
To see additional Britannica Educational Publishing titles, go to rosenpublishing.com.

First Edition

Britannica Educational Publishing
J.E. Luebering: Director, Core Reference Group
Anthony L. Green: Editor, Compton's by Britannica

Rosen Publishing
John Kemmerer: Executive Editor
Jacob R. Steinberg: Editor
Nelson Sá: Art Director
Nicole Russo: Designer
Cindy Reiman: Photography Manager

Library of Congress Cataloging-in-Publication Data

Burshtein, Karen.
Lionel Messi: soccer's top scorer/Karen Burshtein.—First Edition.
    pages cm.—(Living Legends of Sports)
Includes bibliographical references and index.
ISBN 978-1-68048-129-7 (Library bound)—ISBN 978-1-68048-130-3 (Paperback)—ISBN 978-1-68048-132-7 (6-pack)
1. Messi, Lionel, 1987- —Juvenile literature. 2. Soccer players—Argentina—Biography—Juvenile literature. I. Title.
GV942.7.M398B87 2015
796.334092—dc23
[B]
    2014041864

Manufactured in the United States of America

Photo credits: Cover, pp. 1, 36–37 Josep Lago/AFP/Getty Images; pp. 4, 7, 22–23, 30–31 © AP Images; p. 6 Belgrano; p. 8 © wareham.nl (sport)/Alamy; p. 10 Lluis Gene/AFP/Getty Images; p. 13 Rex Features/AP Images; p. 14 Maxisport/Shutterstock.com; p. 15 Natursports/Shutterstock.com; p. 17 Javier Soriano/AFP/Getty Images; p. 19 Kyodo/AP Images; pp. 24–25 AGIF/Shutterstock.com; pp. 26–27 Quique Garcia/AFP/Getty Images; pp. 28–29, 39 David Ramos/Getty Images; p. 33 Chen Shaojin/Xinhua/Landov; pp. 34–35 Juan Mabromata/AFP/Getty Images; p. 40 Emka74/Shutterstock.com; cover and interior pages background images © iStockphoto.com/traffic_analyzer (soccer field illustration), © iStockphoto.com/Nikada (texture).

CONTENTS

INTRODUCTION

Soccer is by far the world's most popular team sport. Part of that popularity comes from how little equipment is needed to start a game. With just a ball and goal posts (even improvised ones) you can get a game of soccer going pretty much anywhere. This is an important consideration in many less economically developed countries where kids may not have access to expensive clubhouses or sporting equipment.

In Argentina, a soccer player named Lionel Messi showed many of the traits of a standout player from an early age. Among these

In an April 2011 match, Lionel Messi dazzled fans at the Camp Nou stadium in Barcelona, Spain, with his fancy footwork and superb control of the ball—skills that have made him a living legend of soccer.

traits are the intelligence and the athleticism that soccer demands. Also notable is that Messi overcame physical difficulties as a young man and later dominated the sport and surpassed his peers. Today, he is a living legend.

Messi plays forward on both Argentina's national team and for FC Barcelona, a popular team in Spain. His coach has called him the "Michael Jordan of soccer"—a player capable of defining an era. Many sports critics even suggest that he may be the best soccer player of all time. He is a skilled playmaker and a thoughtful team player. To be at the top of one of the most popular sports in the world is a big honor but also carries with it huge pressure and responsibility. At only twenty-seven years old, Messi wears these pressures on his shoulders as ably as he handles the ball with his feet.

QUICK **FACT**

Outside of the United States and Canada, soccer is commonly known as football or association football. The word *soccer* **was originally derived from an abbreviation of the word** *association* **in** *association football.*

CHAPTER ONE

The Early Years

Soccer is in Argentina's roots, and it is the country's most beloved sport. Most Argentines play soccer from a young age, and many dream of becoming a big league soccer player. Born on June 24, 1987, Lionel Andrés Messi Cuccittini (nicknamed "Leo") was no exception.

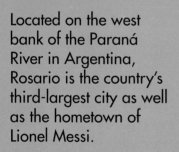

Located on the west bank of the Paraná River in Argentina, Rosario is the country's third-largest city as well as the hometown of Lionel Messi.

As a young child, Leo grew up in the river port city of Rosario, Argentina's third-largest city. Leo's father, Jorge Horacio Messi, was a steelworker. His mother, Celia María Cuccittini, worked part-time as a cleaner. Both parents were of Italian origin—as is a good portion of the population of Argentina. Leo was the Messis' third child after older brothers Rodrigo and Matías. His younger sister, María Sol, was born when Leo was eight years old.

Fancy Footwork at a Young Age

Like many Argentine children, the Messi boys looked up to Diego Maradona. Maradona was a superstar of Argentine soccer. In the quarterfinal of the 1986 World Cup, he scored the famous "Hand of God" goal—he illegally hit the ball with his hand, but the referee mistakenly thought he had used his head (which is allowed). After scoring another spectacular goal four minutes later, Argentina won the match.

Argentine soccer superstar Diego Maradona is shown here celebrating his country's victory at the 1986 World Cup. Maradona is considered a hero by many Argentine fans of soccer and an inspiration for amateur soccer players.

QUICK FACT

His first big fan, Leo's grandmother later passed away when he was only ten years old. To this day, every time Leo scores a goal he points to the sky in a salute to his grandmother.

Leo started playing soccer at the age of five. He would follow his brothers to the pitch where Grandoli, the local soccer club, played. At first Leo would kick soccer balls against a wall and imitate the moves of the older boys. However, eventually some of the coaches noticed his flair and effectiveness. They asked him why he didn't join in with the older boys, despite his smaller size.

Leo didn't shy away from the challenge. This was in part due to his grandmother's encouragement. She would convince the coaches to play Leo (who was small even for his young age) against the biggest of the boys.

By age eight, Leo had joined the youth team of Newell's Old Boys, a Rosario-based, top-division soccer club. There he started to show the

Estadio Marcelo A. Bielsa, in Rosario, Argentina, is the home of the Newell's Old Boys soccer club, where Messi began playing in the youth division at age eight.

BIENVENIDOS A LA CASA DEL CAMPEON

CLUB ATLETICO NEWELL'S OLD BOYS

6 PLATEAS SECTOR
A·B·C·D·E·F·G

phenomenal skills that made him a handful for any opposing team. The masterly way he worked the ball with either foot, his strength, and his playmaking all made him a key player. Leo already showed many signs of the Messi that is well known today.

Finding His Way Off the Field

While he excelled as a soccer player, Messi recalls feeling at home and comfortable only on the soccer pitch. He was shy to the point of being almost entirely silent. At school he would have his friends raise their hands to ask questions for him. He didn't show much interest in activities other than soccer. For example, he did not read much, and as an adult he admits that he has read very few books cover to cover. Family, friends, and fútbol ("soccer" in Spanish) seemed to be his main interests. As well as food.

As an adult Messi says he is encouraged to excel at soccer out of his desire to challenge himself and improve at the sport. However, as a child, sweet treats were Leo's incentive, especially his favorite: *alfajores*. *Alfajores* are a sugary, Argentine cookie. Once his coach promised him one *alfajor* for each goal that he scored. Leo remembers scoring five or six goals after that promise.

Despite his quiet personality off the pitch, Leo was dazzling his country. He was the best player on "La Máquina del 87," the youth section of Newell's Old Boys soccer club that won four championships in six years. Big clubs nationwide were already starting to pay attention to him. Leo's father managed his blooming career.

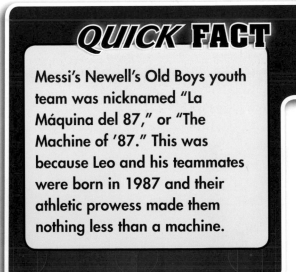

QUICK FACT

Messi's Newell's Old Boys youth team was nicknamed "La Máquina del 87," or "The Machine of '87." This was because Leo and his teammates were born in 1987 and their athletic prowess made them nothing less than a machine.

Popularity Abroad

Leo's popularity as a child wasn't limited to Argentina. Prestigious clubs in other countries were noticing him, too. This would prove helpful when, at age eleven, Leo was diagnosed with growth hormone deficiency—a biological condition that leads to short height and dwarfism.

Leo's small size has always been apparent. Once he was diagnosed, his family knew that his condition could become debilitating and affect his strength and his stamina. His parents started him on a growth hormone treatment that doctors recommended, but after several months they could no longer afford the cost of treatment.

The FC Barcelona youth club in Barcelona, Spain, was one of the teams that had kept an eye on Leo. They arranged a deal with the Messi family wherein the team would cover the costs of Leo's treatment if Leo committed to play for their team. Thus, at the age of twelve in 2000, Leo joined FC Barcelona's under-14 team, La Masia.

Here Lionel Messi participates in a training session for La Masia in 2005. That same year, Messi had become the youngest player on FC Barcelona's team to score a goal in a youth division game, bringing him into the public spotlight.

The Messi family uprooted to Spain, settling in Barcelona. The move was hard for Leo. He missed home and killed time off the field sleeping, playing video games, or hanging out with his family. Nevertheless, FC Barcelona kept him busy as they fostered him through their youth academy at a dizzying speed. He scored 21 goals in 14 games for the junior team, rising quickly through Barcelona's higher rank youth teams—the junior Infantil B and Cadete B and A teams. At age sixteen he made his informal debut with FC Barcelona in a friendly match against FC Porto, a competing team from neighboring Portugal.

QUICK FACT

La Liga is the first division of the National Professional Football League in Spain. Founded in 1929, it consists of twenty teams, but it is without a doubt dominated by Real Madrid and FC Barcelona.

Moving forward Leo began gathering the milestones that would characterize him as a player. He became the youngest player ever to score in a La Liga division game for Barcelona on May 1, 2005. He was just seventeen years old.

As a teenager Leo accomplished his early success with a calmness and sense of purpose that would be the envy of anyone in his profession. Furthermore, Leo's rise to success didn't bring him to bad habits or a sense of entitlement. He remained focused as he continued his climb to the top of the world of soccer.

CHAPTER TWO

FC Barcelona and the Argentine National Team

The short, floppy-haired Lionel Messi perhaps looked more like a member of a boy band than a soccer star when he became a member of FC Barcelona. His size earned him the nickname "La Pulga" ("The Flea" in Spanish). However, on the field Leo commanded respect. By the end of his first season with Barça—as FC Barcelona is colloquially known—the whole soccer world was talking about his astonishing skills. Naturally left-footed, quick, and in total control of the ball, Leo was a keen passer who could easily thread his way through packed defenses. Finding open spaces that others couldn't see was just one of the many tricks in his bag.

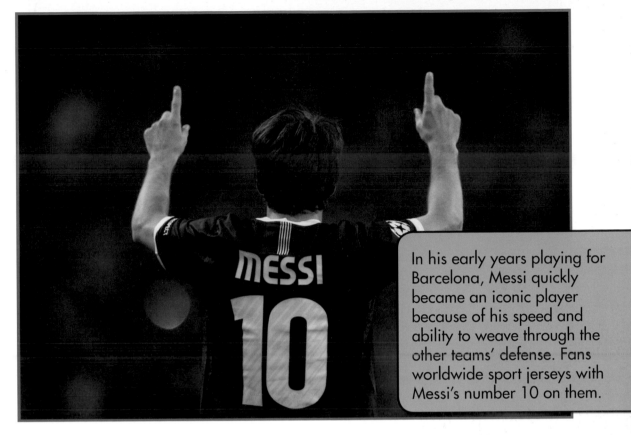

In his early years playing for Barcelona, Messi quickly became an iconic player because of his speed and ability to weave through the other teams' defense. Fans worldwide sport jerseys with Messi's number 10 on them.

In the words of his former coach at FC Barcelona, Pep Guardiola, Messi was "the best player in absolutely every facet . . . I am sorry for those who want to dethrone him, but he is simply different from all the rest."

In 2005 Messi was granted Spanish citizenship. It was an honor greeted with mixed feelings by the proud local Catalan supporters of FC Barcelona, but that allowed Messi to play soccer in La Liga. Messi learned basic Catalan, the language of that region of Spain. In interviews and in

QUICK FACT

Popularly known as Barça, FC Barcelona is known for its players' skillful and entertaining style of play that is called *tiki-taka*, which emphasizes passing and artful flowing movement. Barcelona's stadium, Camp Nou, is one of the most recognizable stadium names in the world.

Former FC Barcelona coach and Messi's mentor Pep Guardiola has compared Lionel Messi to Michael Jordan in terms of being an iconic sports player. Guardiola believes Messi could well be the best soccer player of all time.

QUICK FACT

Founded in 1899, Barça has been seen as a major expression of Catalan identity dating back to the military dictatorship of Francisco Franco (which lasted from 1939 to 1975), who prohibited the use of the Catalan language and suppressed Catalan culture.

public, Messi is too shy to speak Catalan, but in post-game victories he has often shouted FC Barcelona's famous slogan: *"Visca el Barça i visca Catalunya!"* ("Long live Barça and long live Catalonia!"), along with his teammates and their fans.

The Soccer Wiz

As a player for Barça, Messi collected dazzling landmarks. In 2006, Barcelona won the UEFA Champions League (the European

Lionel Messi shows his FIFA Ballon D'Or Award to his supporters at Camp Nou, Barcelona, in 2011. He had also won the trophy in 2009 and 2010, and would again win the award in 2012.

club championship) title. By 2008, Messi was Barcelona's leading goal scorer. His 2008–9 season was particularly memorable as Messi helped Barcelona win the club's first "treble" (or winning three major European club trophies in one season). Messi alone scored 38 goals in 51 matches that season. During the 2009–10 season, he scored 34 goals in domestic games. Barcelona once again was the La Liga champion.

Messi also made major achievements independent of his team's wins. He earned the Golden Shoe Award as Europe's leading scorer and was also named FIFA's World Player of the Year in 2009. Again in 2010, 2011, and 2012, Messi won FIFA's World Player of the Year award, which had been renamed the FIFA Ballon d'Or in 2010. Thus Messi became the first player to win the coveted award four years in a row.

The 2011–12 season was probably Messi's best. In March 2012 he netted his 233rd goal for Barcelona, becoming the club's all-time leading scorer at only twenty-four years old. He finished that season with 73 goals in all competitions, more than any other player had accomplished in a single season in history.

Team Argentina, Too

While Messi was already racking up his accomplishments with Barça, Argentina had quickly signed him up for their own national team in 2005. He would soon be showing off his flair playing for his home country as well in international matches, displaying what Argentines call *gambeta*: the skilled high-speed dribble with the flourish of a tango step. It was a talent for which Messi's idol Maradona was also known.

In June 2005, Argentina's under-20 team, with Messi on the field, became champions in the FIFA World Youth Championship. He was voted Player of the Tournament after securing Argentina's victory over Nigeria with a pair of penalty kicks.

Messi was also on Argentina's 2006 World Cup team, though at only eighteen, he spent most of his time on the bench. However, by the 2008 Beijing Olympic Games, he was on the field often enough to help Argentina win the gold medal. By 2010, Messi was already

Argentina's Lionel Messi drives the ball during the 2010 World Cup quarterfinal match against Germany in Cape Town, South Africa, in July 2010.

the well-known superstar of Barça when he also helped the national Argentine team make it to the quarterfinals at the World Cup in South Africa.

Messi's efforts on the Argentine national team won him Argentina's Sports Journalist Association "Olimpia de Plata" Footballer of the Year award several years over.

Barcelona Leo vs. Argentine Leo

In spite of his many awards with the Argentine national team, Lionel Messi is not as popular in his home country as he is in the rest of the world. One major criticism that makes Messi less popular among Argentines is that his accomplishments with the Argentine team don't measure up to those he has made with FC Barcelona.

It is natural that Messi's dynamic with his Argentine teammates would be different from the one that he has with the Barcelona team. For one, Messi was formed from a young age at La Masia, FC Barcelona's youth academy, with many of the same players with whom he came to play on the adult team. The teammates knew each other's moves from a young age.

According to Messi, he neither does nor would he change his playing style for either team. He also believes that his style and practice with Barcelona will eventually pay off on the field with Argentina. He has claimed in interviews that it is just a question of continuing to work with the Argentine team to develop a deeper understanding of each other's styles and to develop confidence together as a great team. At the 2014 World Cup in Brazil, Leo scored four goals and almost single-handedly moved Argentina through the early group stage and knockout stages. Messi scored crucial goals against Bosnia-Herzegovina, Nigeria, and Iran, bringing Argentina to the final match. Argentina lost the final 1–0 to Germany, but Messi nevertheless won the Golden Ball award as the tournament's best player.

Despite the honor, many commentators noted the disappointment on Messi's face as he was handed his trophy. He wanted a win for his

At the 2014 World Cup Final in Rio de Janeiro, Brazil, on July 13, 2014, Germany beat Argentina 1–0. Nonetheless, Lionel Messi won the Ballon D'Or trophy for the World Cup's best player. While Messi accepted his individual award, his face showed his disappointment at Argentina losing the final.

whole Argentine team, a World Cup—the one trophy so far not in his collection. "I prefer to win titles with the team before individual prizes or outscoring everyone," he said after the Cup.

The many expectations of his teams, fans around the world, fellow Argentines, and the media put a lot of pressure on Messi's shoulders. He has largely learned to overcome that, but he claims he is still concerned with the pressure that he puts on himself. In a January 2013 interview for *World Soccer*, Messi said, "I'm more critical with myself than anyone else is. I know when I have done well and when I have done badly. I don't need anyone to tell me."

CHAPTER THREE

Messi's Influence on Soccer

Even if you add up all the components of Lionel Messi's game—his physical grace, power, and mental agility and his abilities to run faster with the ball than without it and to score goals seemingly almost at will—there is still a mysterious quality to his genius.

The most gifted sports commentators have had trouble finding the right words to describe what makes Messi such a great player. This is often the case with someone who has an exceptional talent. The answer that most fans and commentators offer is that Messi has a natural, God-given gift, and his wild success cannot otherwise be explained. His coach once said those wanting to understand Messi's talent simply must watch him play.

Don't ask Messi himself either. Reporters have said interviews with the soccer superstar are difficult and that getting Messi to talk about his own talent or success is like pulling teeth.

The usually shy Messi faces reporters ahead of a training session for Argentina's national soccer team at the 2008 Olympics in China.

Proving His Endurance

Surprising as it may sound, Messi's childhood growth hormone deficiency was likely a factor in making him the soccer genius that he later became. At a young age, he learned how to play against bigger and stronger opponents—a lesson that stayed with him. After completing growth hormone treatment, Messi grew to his full height of 5'7", but nobody could deny that the young player had overcome a very difficult trial so early in his career. This endurance through difficult times has become one of Messi's most discussed qualities.

When Messi was first signed to Barcelona's La Masia youth academy, his peers thought they would quickly wipe him off the field because of his height. Through growth hormone treatments and the superior sportsmanship that he developed, Messi proved them very wrong. "La Pulga" may

After years of difficulty, Lionel Messi earned his standing at the top of the sport. Here he darts around an opponent during the 2014 World Cup semifinals game between Argentina and the Netherlands in São Paulo, Brazil.

have sounded belittling, but like a flea, Messi wasn't just small—he was also hard to shake off.

Greatest Player of All Time?

A popular debate among contemporary soccer fans is to discuss Lionel Messi's ultimate place in the sports history books. Many ask, "Will he be thought of as the greatest player of all time?" Plenty of fellow soccer players seem to think so. So do the many fans who see his love for the game each time he takes to the field. After all that he has already achieved, Messi continues to express in interviews that he can improve in all aspects of his game.

Many critics say that until Messi has won a FIFA World Cup, he can't be regarded as this generation's best soccer player. Others yet say that Messi doesn't need a World Cup win to be considered the best, as his collective time

QUICK FACT

Every sport has its archrivals. In soccer many compare Lionel Messi to Cristiano Ronaldo, the Portuguese forward for Real Madrid. Both are considered to be the most gifted soccer players of their generation.

outside that competition amount to an outstanding achievement. After the 2014 World Cup, sports journalist Lee Roden wrote, "If Messi is to be considered among the greatest ever to play the game…120 minutes isolated from thousands shouldn't be enough to overshadow a lengthy career at the highest level."

Messi has expressed a similar opinion at times. One of his own idols, Alfredo di Stéfano, an Argentine-Spanish soccer star of the 1950s, never won a World Cup, and Messi insists that no one

Lionel Messi and Portuguese star Cristiano Ronaldo (who plays forward for Real Madrid, FC Barcelona's main Spanish league rival) have long fought for the title of best soccer player in the public's eye. Here, the rival players are shown in an El Clásico match in Barcelona on October 26, 2013.

Messi and his teammates celebrate their victory during a La Liga match between FC Barcelona and Sevilla FC in Barcelona on November 22, 2014. Messi is known for his superior sportsmanship and for his close relationship with teammates.

would claim that Di Stéfano wasn't one of the greatest. By the same token Messi also insists that he still has time to achieve his dream of winning a World Cup with Argentina and promises that he will do everything possible to see that that happens.

Sportsmanship Above Skills

Beyond his superb skills, Messi wants history to remember him in other, more modest ways, too. In a September 2012 interview with *El País*, Messi said, "My hope is that when I retire that I'm remembered as a good guy. I like to score goals, but I also like to be friends with the people I play with." This is one of the predominant reasons that Lionel Messi is considered a role model for young aspiring soccer players: his emphasis on teamwork and sportsmanship is as apparent as his never-say-die attitude.

After his 2014 World Cup loss, most fans recognized that, at only twenty-seven years of age at the time, Messi still had a long career ahead of him. Messi himself has said that as long as he enjoys the game and finds ways to improve, he will keep on playing. As he matures, his game continues to change. At the beginning of his career, Messi might have been a bit more individualistic and occasionally guilty of ignoring better placed teammates. But as his career progressed, in addition to scoring, he became known for setting up a lot of goals with clever passes that found teammates in the perfect positions.

Former FC Barcelona player, Zlatan Ibrahimović is shown here celebrating with Messi during a La Liga match in Zaragoza, Spain, on March 21, 2010.

QUICK FACT

Matches between FC Barcelona and Real Madrid are called El Clásico. In the March 2014 Clásico, an estimated 400 million viewers worldwide watched—more than three times as many as the global Super Bowl audience that year!

Messi has shown that he can be a generous teammate. In one game against Real Zaragoza, Messi had already scored a hat trick—the soccer term for scoring three goals in one game—and had a chance for a fourth goal. Instead he passed the ball to his then teammate Zlatan Ibrahimović, because, in Messi's own words, "Ibra needed a goal."

Off the Field

Lionel Messi's influence stretches much further than his importance to soccer alone. As one of the most popular sports figures in the world, he knows he has a responsibility to the public. Off the field, Messi does a lot of charity work. He also has a family and a handful of major business endeavors.

Leo Messi Foundation

Messi has always recognized that he was given great opportunities at a young age, and he wants the same for as many kids as possible. In 2007, Messi founded the Leo Messi Foundation to help at-risk children. Its motto is "Choose to believe."

The inspiration for the foundation came after Messi visited a group of sick children in a hospital and seeing how much the presence of somebody that they admired could improve their mood and their will to fight their illness. Messi saw how the visit could give hope to a child—something not always offered by medicine.

Messi poses with a fan in Doha, Qatar, in May 2013, following a ceremony announcing the Leo Messi Foundation's initiative to support mobile health clinics for children in the Middle East, North Africa, and Southeast Asia.

Another of the foundation's goals is to fight against poverty like that which Messi saw growing up in Argentina. Messi saw so many children, even very young ones, who thought they had no choice but to beg on the street or to go off to work. The Leo Messi Foundation helps raise money for and awareness about child poverty and at-risk children, and finding solutions to fight it.

A Better Future for Children

In 2010, Leo became a UNICEF Goodwill Ambassador. In that post he began doing various humanitarian missions across the globe, focusing on children's rights and trying to get children off the streets and out of a life of child labor through education and sports. For example, in his first year as an ambassador he visited Haiti six months after a devastating earthquake had done massive damage to the small island country. He

Part of Messi's motivation to do charity work came from seeing poverty-stricken children living in poor neighborhoods (or, shantytowns) such as this one in Buenos Aires. One of his foundation's goals is to provide less fortunate children with a better future through sports and education.

wanted to help lift people's spirits, especially Haitian children. He also hoped to draw the world's attention to the challenges that these children faced after the earthquake. Messi also met with Argentine troops stationed as part of a UN relief mission to the nation.

In 2013, Messi and his FC Barcelona teammates visited the Middle East, an area of the world that experiences great political tension. During Barça's "Peace Tour," the team met with both Israeli and Palestinian leaders. They also hosted training and matches with Israeli and Palestinian youth, all in the aim of improving often-tense relations between Israel and Palestine.

QUICK FACT

Barça fan clubs aren't just in Barcelona. There are over 1,500 Barça fan clubs throughout the world.

Lionel Messi poses with a group of children after being appointed a UNICEF Goodwill Ambassador at the Camp Nou stadium in Barcelona on March 11, 2010.

While typically shy, Messi comes out of his shell when instructing young children. He has told interviewers that his greatest joy is making a child happy.

Leo Messi: Just Like You and Me?

While Lionel Messi is possibly one of the most famous people in the world, Messi insists that he is a normal person with the same life as anyone else. Off the field, it is almost believable. In 2009, Messi began dating his girlfriend, Antonella Roccuzzo, his best friend's cousin who is also from his hometown of Rosario. On November 2, 2012, the couple gave birth to a son, Thiago. Messi commemorated the event by having his son's name and birthdate stitched onto his soccer cleats.

Despite all that he has achieved in sports, Messi insists that his biggest achievement in life is Thiago. Since Thiago's birth, Messi has explained in many interviews how his son changed his life and priorities, and even how he behaves as a soccer star. When things don't go well on the field, instead of stewing in his disappointment, Messi says he goes home, sees his son, and quickly gets over it.

QUICK FACT

At just a few days old, Thiago Messi was made an honorary member of Newell Old Boys, the Argentine youth club where Messi played before moving to Spain.

Balancing Big Endorsements and a Normal Life

Messi's 2014 revised contract with FC Barcelona, which lasts through 2018, is worth about $27 million a season. The star earns many millions more from endorsements for brands such as Adidas, PepsiCo, Gillette, and Electronic Arts. His total salary for 2014 was estimated to be more than $60 million.

Proud dad Lionel Messi holds his young son, Thiago, in 2013 ahead of a match in Barcelona. Thiago wears a custom Barcelona jersey with the Spanish word *Papi* (or, "daddy") inscribed on the back where Messi's name would normally appear.

Pepsi is just one of the many brands with which Messi has lucrative endorsement deals since becoming a soccer superstar.

Messi still spends a lot of time with his siblings and parents. His father continues to manage his soccer career. His friends, as one might expect, are mostly fellow soccer players. When he returns to Rosario off-season, he hangs out with his old friends from the "Máquina '87" soccer team. In Europe, his closest friends are the soccer stars that he first played with on the under-14 team at La Masia, such as Cesc Fàbregas, Sergio Agüero, and Gerard Piqué. They often insist that, despite his enormous success, "Leo" is the same shy, humble guy that he was when they first met as kids.

Nobody knows for sure how long Messi's career will last. Messi has said, "I have enjoyed it since I was a little boy. When I stop enjoying it, I will stop playing." But chances are that the determined and dedicated sports hero will keep going for a while to come as he tries to score the one thing missing from his long list of achievements—a World Cup title. And, as he does, his scores of fans will continue watching and learning from this sports legend both on and off the field.

TIMELINE

1987 Lionel Messi is born in Rosario, Argentina, on June 24.

1995 Messi joins Newell's Old Boys, a famous youth soccer club in Rosario.

1998 Messi is diagnosed with a growth hormone deficiency.

1999 Messi moves to Barcelona, Spain, with his family to join La Masia, FC Barcelona's youth academy, as well as receive treatment for his medical condition.

2005 Messi becomes a full player for FC Barcelona and the youngest player ever to score in a La Liga division game for the team.

2005 Messi signs on to Argentina's national soccer team.

2007 Messi establishes the Leo Messi Foundation, a charity seeking to provide education and health care to vulnerable children.

2008 Messi helps win the gold medal for Argentina's team at the Beijing Summer Olympic Games.

2009 Messi leads FC Barcelona to a string of important victories including the Champions League, La Liga, and Spanish Super Cup titles.

2009 Messi wins his first FIFA World Player of the Year (later called the Ballon d'Or) award. He takes home the award again in 2010, 2011, and 2012, a record four consecutive times.

2010 Messi becomes a Goodwill Ambassador for UNICEF, supporting children's rights globally.

2012 A son, Thiago, is born to Messi and his partner, Antonella Roccuzzo, on November 2.

2013 Messi and FC Barcelona hold a series of soccer camps in Israel and Palestine to promote cooperation and peace.

2014 In March Messi sets the new Barcelona goal record when he scores his 370th goal as a member of the team.

2014 In July Messi is awarded the Golden Ball, for most valuable player at the World Cup in Brazil.

2015 Messi leads FC Barcelona to the Champions League final.

Pelé (1940–) is one of the most famous soccer players of all time. Pelé is known as an ambassador of the sport. He was part of the Brazilian national teams that won three World Cup championships in 1958, 1962, and 1970.

Johan Cruyff (1947–) is a Dutch forward known for his imaginative playmaking and consistent goal scoring. Cruyff led the Netherlands national team to the finals of the 1974 World Cup.

Diego Maradona (1960–) is an Argentine-born legend and generally regarded as the best soccer player of the 1980s. He played for FC Barcelona as well as his national team. He is known for the legendary and controversial "Hand of God" goal at the 1986 World Cup.

Mia Hamm (1972–) is an American soccer player who became the first female international star of the sport. She starred on the U.S. national team that won World Cup championships in 1991 and 1999 and Olympic gold medals in 1996 and 2004. She is a two-time FIFA World Player of the Year winner.

David Beckham (1975–) is the one-time captain of the U.K. team who gained international fame for his bending free-kicks. He played with Manchester United and Real Madrid before signing with the L.A. Galaxy for $250 million with the aim of making soccer more popular in the United States.

Cristiano Ronaldo (1985–) is a Portuguese forward for Real Madrid, considered to be one of the most gifted young soccer players of his and Lionel Messi's generation.

GLOSSARY

athleticism A show of above average or superior athletic ability.

Ballon d'Or A French phrase meaning "Golden Ball" that is the name of the award given by FIFA each year to the soccer player who is considered to have performed the best the previous year.

Catalonia A region in northeastern Spain known for its distinct culture and language. Its capital city is Barcelona.

economically developing country A country whose economy, or organization of money, goods, and trade, is less developed but may be improving.

FIFA Abbreviation for the Fédération Internationale de Football Association (French for "The International Federation of Association Football"), the international governing organization of soccer founded in 1904.

group stage The initial stage in FIFA soccer tournaments in which teams are separated into groups and play each team within their group before the winning teams advance to further rounds.

growth hormone deficiency A biological condition in which the body does not produce sufficient growth hormones, leading to short stature and dwarfism.

header A soccer move in which a player's head connects with a ball that is in the air.

humanitarian mission A trip made by an individual or group to provide emergency help to a country or population affected by natural, political, or social hardship.

playmaker In soccer, the person who sets up plays, usually by controlling the flow of a team's offensive play and who is often involved in passing the ball in a move that leads to goals.

tango A ballroom dance of Latin American origin to music in 2/4 time and marked by pauses between steps and a variety of body postures.

UNICEF Abbreviation for the United Nations International Children's Emergency Fund, a United Nations program that provides relief and assistance to children in need in developing countries.

FOR MORE INFORMATION

Books

Hollar, Sherman. *Soccer and Its Greatest Players.* New York, NY: Britannica Educational Publishing, 2011.

Jökulsson, Illugi. *Messi* (World Soccer Legends). New York, NY: Abbeville Press, 2014.

Morgan, Alex. *Saving the Team.* New York, NY: Simon & Schuster Books for Young Readers, 2013.

Part, Michael. *The Flea: The Amazing Story of Leo Messi.* Beverly Hills, CA: Sole Books, 2013.

Perez, Mike. *Lionel Messi: The Ultimate Fan Book.* London, UK: Carlton Publishing, 2014.

Websites

Because of the changing nature of Internet links, Rosen Publishing has developed an online list of websites related to the subject of this book. This site is updated regularly. Please use this link to access the list:

http://www.rosenlinks.com/LLS/Messi

INDEX